WOULD YOU LIKE A PUPPY?

SOMEONE YOU CAN LOVE AND WHO LOVES YOU?

OU CAN HAVE A WELL-TRAINED DOG . . .

. . . WHO WILL BE YOUR PLAYMATE.

OULDN'T IT BE FUN TO HAVE YOUR VERY OWN DOG TRAVEL
HEREVER YOU GO . . .

. . . AND GROW TO BE A GOOD WORKER? IT'S EASY FOR YOU AND A PUP TO LEARN.

KID'S DOG

KID'S DOG
A Training Book
Richard A. Wolters

DOUBLEDAY & COMPANY, INC.
GARDEN CITY, NEW YORK 1978

for Benjamin, my favorite kid,
and Tar, my favorite dog

Library of Congress Cataloging in Publication Data

Wolters, Richard A
    Kid's dog.

    Includes index.
    SUMMARY: Instructions for training a new puppy including
chapters on commands, housebreaking, and walking on a leash.
    1. Dogs—Training—Juvenile literature. [1. Dogs—Training] I. Title.
SF431.W676   636.7′08′87
ISBN 0-385-11550-4 Trade
        0-385-11551-2 Prebound
Library of Congress Catalog Card Number 76–23803

Contents

KID'S DOG

What You Should Know About Man's and Woman's Best Friend

It has always been said that the dog is man's best friend. It's true, but humans have been good friends of the dogs too. The friendship began many thousands of years ago when one of our early ancestors, let's call him Mr. Stone Age, invited dogs to come live with him in his cave. This might not have happened if old Uncle Stony had longer legs and if his nose and ears worked better. As it turned out, Uncle learned that he needed the dog to help him catch supper. At that time the only way to get food was to hunt with a spear. The dog was better than Uncle Stony at scenting and trailing game. Uncle ran on two legs; even a small dog on four legs was swifter than Uncle Stony. To make sure he got supper, Uncle teamed up with the dog. They became partners. They shared the catch. Uncle got the meat and the dog got the bones. There was another reason for Uncle inviting the dog to join

15

the Stone Age family, to live in the cave and be given a place to bed down next to the fire. The dog's hearing was much better than the cave man's. Uncle Stony soon learned that the dog would bark and give an early warning if some furious animal were sneaking around at night to make his dinner out of him or one of his children. For his work the dog got supper and a warm bed. Uncle got supper and good protection. Man and dog lived together happily forever after.

Puppies were some of the first "toys" that Uncle Stony's children and grandchildren had. When the family grew and moved out of the caves, they took the dogs with them. The dogs even helped them move. They pulled the family possessions on sled-like carts. Wherever early man went in his travels, over the far corners of the world, he took his dogs with him and they learned new tasks. Some of Mr. Stone Age's relatives became farmers. The dogs were taught to herd the farm animals. The dogs were bred to do all kinds of jobs. They pulled sleds in lands where there was snow. When the wheel was invented, they pulled carts. They swam net lines across rivers to catch fish. Some were bred to chase running game, and others were taught to hunt only birds. Some were trained to keep rats away from the house, some to dig up vegetables. Some dogs were bred to stay small, like toys, to be companions to the family. The important thing was, for all those thousands of years, dogs had work to do.

Many of the wild animals, like the dinosaur, who were roaming around Uncle Stony's family have become extinct. They have all died out. Many people today feel that this might have happened to man too had it not been for help from the dog. Uncle and his family were not very ferocious. Man didn't seem to be much of a match for his enemies. He did not have horns to fight with, not even a sharp hoof for kicking. He couldn't run as fast as most animals, his skin was very soft and could be punctured easily. Early man did not have fangs or poisonous stingers. His bite wasn't even as good as that of a small Pekingese pup. Why did man survive? Why did he win over all the others in the animal kingdom? The other animals had to spend all their time searching for food. With the help of the dog, early man became such a good hunter that he had time to think about other things. He learned how to use his hands. Men like Mr. Stone Age started to figure out how to make tools and use them. This all might not have happened without the protection and the work that the dog did. It took thousands of years, but man slowly developed and built our civilization.

Today if we want to see all the different animals that live in the world, we can go to the zoo. But the dog won't be shown there. He doesn't live there. He lives in our houses. What started out as a very simple life in Uncle Stony's time has changed. We now have towns and cities, automobiles, television, airplanes, rockets, and all the other things you know about plus a distant relative of Uncle's old friend, the dog. Man and dog have stayed friends a long time.

Things have changed for the dog, too. Although there are hundreds of different breeds today, very few of them are workers. They could be, but there is not much work for most of them. Most people work in a plant, a factory, an office, or a store. And you know there is very little a dog can do there. Even on the farms today the work is done by machinery. Of the millions of dogs in this country, few have jobs. There are very few sled dogs. None help the fisherman by swimming the net lines. With the automobile, who needs a dog to pull a cart? Few dogs are used to herd sheep. Dogs are used by the hunter today both to find and retrieve game, but not many people hunt for their food. Most of the hunting today takes place in the supermarket where your mother hunts for food at a price she can afford to pay. The dogs that are doing an important job today are those being trained to lead blind people. They do fine work. They are good citizens.

Everyone agrees that a student who works and does his job in school is happier than one who doesn't. In that way, dogs are no different from kids.

What happens to most dogs who live with us today? Since there is no real job around the house for them to do, most grow up without any education. Dogs who go untrained are not very different from kids who become school dropouts.

They get into mischief. There are too many dogs in our communities that are pests, not pets.

Do you know how most of the dogs are obtained in this country? The kids beg their dad for a pup. He finally agrees. Mom asks, "Who is going to take care of the dog?" The kids all say that they will. What happens in most homes is that after a few months the kids forget to take care of the dog and Mom has to do it. Dad is away most of the day, Mom is very busy, and the kids are off at school. No one really takes the time to learn how to train Fido. The dog will learn by himself. Most of the things he learns that way do not make him a very good member of the family or the neighborhood. People say, "That neighbor's dog is a pain."

A well-mannered dog, like a well-behaved kid, is a joy to have around. It is very easy to train a dog. It only takes a few minutes a day. A well-trained dog only has to learn the meaning of about six words. Like no other animal, one thing comes built into every puppy when he is born—he wants to please his master. If a pupil wants to please the teacher, he will do well in school, and that is the way it is with the dog. Cats are very independent. It's very hard to train them. Because dogs and man have worked together for so long, dogs have come to depend on people. They are easy to train.

A pup wants to please. Let him know you love him.

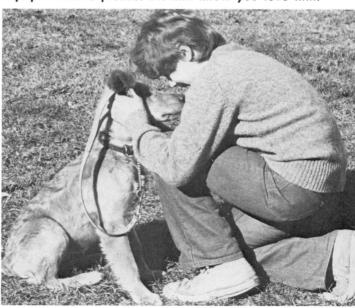

Training

The way a dog is trained is not very different from the way you are trained. If you like your teacher, you will try to be a good student. So the first thing you have to do is to make the pup like you. This is very easy. The nature of a dog is friendly. He'll like you from the very beginning. That is one reason training should start very early. You would not expect a kid to start school at age sixteen, when he's almost grown. The same is true for the dog. Since we will start the training at a very early age, it will mean that the pup will come to your house to live when he is only seven weeks old. At that age there should be no problem getting the pup to like you. As the master, you will take the place of the puppy's mother. You will feed him, give him a nice warm bed, keep him clean, and play with him. Can you see any reason why he wouldn't like that? It will be only natural that he will want you as his friend.

There was a little boy who lived down the street from where I live. He got a puppy and I often watched him with his dog. From the very beginning he played too hard with his pup. He wanted to roughhouse, but the pup was too young for that sort of play. Soon, every time the pup saw the boy he'd run off to hide. This made the boy angry, so he went after the dog. Once I saw the boy reach under the porch and drag the pup out by one of his legs. You could not expect a pup to like that kind of treatment. A puppy is just like a little baby. Their bones and muscles are not very strong and they can be hurt easily.

One day I talked to the boy about the way he treated his dog. He was not a mean boy. He just did not understand why his pup would not have any fun with him. We talked about it a long time. When I told him that he would not like it if his parents and teachers treated him that way, his answer startled me. He said, "They're always telling me what I have to do."

This little boy had the feeling that the dog was his plaything. It was his slave, to do with as he wished. He thought he was playing teacher by trying to make the pup do anything he wanted. The boy wanted to give the orders; some children do.

It is easy to see why that puppy would not learn for the boy. It is very important in training a dog to be fair. Training is not only teaching commands. Training is the whole life that you and your dog have together. If you are kind to the dog, the commands will be easy to teach because if he likes you he'll want to please you.

The most important part of training is to be consistent. That means to always do a thing the same way. If a teacher punishes you one day for chewing gum in class and lets you do it the next day, you wouldn't know what to believe. If you are training a dog not to beg from the table while the family is eating, you must never, never, feed him from the table. If you do it once, he will think that you might change your mind and feed him again. He won't know what to believe. In training, you must always do things or repeat things the same way.

You have to make sure in training that the dog knows you mean what you say. If your teacher tells you to do some homework, and you don't do it, and she than says nothing about it, you might not do it the next time she asks. The same thing is true with the dog. For example, after a dog learns the command SIT, you must see to it that he always does it when told to do so. If you do not teach the pup that you mean what you say, he will obey only when he wants to.

Be consistent in the training. A well-mannered pup won't beg from the table. Don't ever feed him at the table.

One thing to always remember in training a dog: there is no need to get angry and shout at the dog. That will not help. The way to make a correction is to quietly do the task over. If your teacher asks you to add a group of numbers and you make a mistake, it will not help if she shouts at you. The best way for you to learn is to do the addition over and see where you made a mistake.

Most important in training is to remember to give the dog praise. A pat on the head and telling him he's a good fellow is what the dog really wants. Learning something and doing the right thing are not always easy. When the dog does the right thing, make sure you let him know that you are pleased. You know how good you feel when your dad says you were good. Make the dog feel good too. Next time he'll do the right thing again. He likes it when you are pleased.

Michele wanted to be friendly but didn't know how to lift the pup . . .

DON'T HURT THE PUP

. . . Eric, her older brother, showed her how. One hand goes under the pup for support, the other on top holds him. The pup likes to be held.

ow everybody is happy. Hurting a pup will frighten him.

Giving Commands

A well-trained and mannered dog has to learn only five or six commands. SIT, STAY, COME, DOWN, HEEL, and one you hear very often yourself, NO. A dog does not understand words and sentences as we do. The dog does not care if you speak to it in French, Chinese, Hebrew, or Spanish. Whatever language is used, the dog will come to learn that one sound means for him to do one thing. You should give commands as two words, starting with the dog's name. His name is also a command. It's the attention command. When your teacher wants to say something important to the class, she will say, "Class!" She will wait for everyone to settle down, then she will start to speak. If she wants to call on one student, she will name the girl or boy to get their attention. It is the same way in training a dog. Call his name and get his attention, then give the command.

Since the dog's name is also a command, you should give the dog a short name like Jock, Ben, Jill, Belle. Sharply call the name, and then in a firm voice give the command. A firm, strong voice is used because you are not asking the dog if he would like to do the command, you are telling him he has to do it. Show him by the tone of your voice that you mean business.

Commands should be the dog's name plus one word, BELLE, SIT, or BELLE, COME. Most people make the mistake of saying too much. Have you ever heard a person talking to his dog like this? "Come on now, Spot, sit . . . no, no, come on, let's try it again. Over here now, sit, Spot. Good fellow . . . I said sit." All that language is going to confuse the dog. In that example the trainer was asking the dog to do one thing, but if you look back and read it, you will see that in all that talk two other commands were given, the words "come" and "no" were used along with the command "sit." How could we expect the dog to understand that kind of language? He can't, so he doesn't know what to do.

Give strong commands. You are not asking the dog to obey, you are telling him that he must. He may not like it but he'll get the idea if you speak in a firm voice. Michele is commanding DOWN. Of course the pup would rather be up with her, but he learned she meant what she said.

They all look alike but they are not.

Selecting a Puppy

Dogs come in all shapes and sizes. Some have long hair, some short, some wire hair, curly hair, and some have no hair. Some are tall, some are short. They come in black, white, brown, blond, red, blue, and all shades of these colors. No matter what the pup looks like, you will fall in love with it. It's a fact that all dogs are cute, cuddly fluffballs when they are puppies. When they grow up, some of them may weigh only six pounds, but others can weigh up to 160 pounds, and that is a lot of dog to play with. Feeding such a big dog could cost as much as it costs to feed you, that is, if you eat well. The decision as to what dog to get should be made by the adults in the family. Let them pick the pup. I'm sure you will love the one they choose. But you should still know about selecting the pup because you can tell your parents what you know about picking a pup.

Purebred dogs cost a lot of money, and spending it is the kind of decision your parents have to make. Should the dog be male or female? Many people who train dogs think the female is easier to handle. She will stay at home. They think she takes to training better. I do not agree completely with this. The right dog from the litter will take to training whether it be a boy or a girl. It is true that the female is a problem twice a year when she comes into season. If she is bred and has pups, that means a lot of extra work.

The advantage of getting a purebred dog is that you will know what size he will grow to be and what he will look like. Here is a list of some of the purebred dogs that have proven to be good with children, and a list that for many reasons are not very good for kids.

Good for Children

American water spaniel
basset hound
beagle
boxer
Brittany spaniel
bulldog
coonhound
English setter

foxhound
golden retriever
great Dane
Irish water
    spaniel
Labrador
    retriever

Old English
    sheepdog
pointer
poodle
    (standard)
springer spaniel

Not Good for Children

American cocker
    spaniel
American toy fox
    terrier
Chesapeake Bay
    retriever
Chihuahua
chow
dachshund
Doberman pinscher

German
    shepherd
husky
Italian greyhound
Japanese spaniel
Kerry blue terrier
Malemute
Maltese terrier
Mexican hairless
miniature pinscher

Pekingese
Pomeranian
Samoyed
Scottish terrier
spitz
toy Manchester
wire-haired fox
    terrier
Yorkshire terrier

There is a lot of new information about selecting a pup and training it that few people pay attention to. Scientists have studied dogs and the family life of puppies and have a lot of new information. They found that a purebred dog with registration papers is no smarter than a mutt, which is a slang name for a mixed breed. The mutt will learn just as fast as any dog.

Picking the right dog from the litter is very important. There is a new test that takes the guesswork out of which pup, of the five or ten in the litter, is the best one. This testing should be done by your parents.* But so you will understand, here is what it is about.

All animals who have many brothers and sisters have to struggle with each other to get their food and attention from their mother. Living in this group, called a litter, is not always easy. Very young pups soon learn who are the strong ones and who are the weaker. Watch a litter of pups and you will see what I mean. Put your hand into the kennel and the strongest will fight his way past his brothers and sisters to get to you. The shy ones will sit back. They will not fight past the strong ones to get to you. The ones that act like little bulls get to the food, and the shy ones, sometimes called wallflowers, get pushed aside. Every litter develops its bulls and its wallflowers. Scientists call this the pecking order. They have found that the pups at both ends of the pecking order, the bulls and the wallflowers, are difficult dogs to train. The dogs who fall somewhere in between the bulls and the wallflowers in the pecking order are the best dogs for training. The Puppy Behavior Test will show where each dog belongs in this pecking order.

Do you know how most pups are picked from the litter? There are two ways. One, the person who is buying the pup falls in love with the cute one who has a spot or mark he or she likes. Two, they take the one that fights its way to the person and licks his face. Neither way has much to do with how well the pup will take to his training. At this early age of only six weeks, the test will show which pups will most

* Puppy Behavior Test. *City Dog*, by Richard A. Wolters.

likely grow to be hardheaded bulls, which will be friendly and nice, and which will be too shy. You are going to have your dog for twelve to fifteen years. You should start out with one that is going to give you the fewest problems.

Of course the dog's health should be considered when you get a pup. He should be taken to a veterinarian as soon as possible. The vet will tell you if the pup is well. He'll give the pup the shots he needs and tell you how much to feed the young dog. There are a few things to look for while selecting the pup. A healthy dog's eyes and nose will not be runny. His teeth will be white, not stained with brown marks. The teeth will be straight. His skin will be soft and his belly button will not be popped out. He will seem lively and full of fun.

Michele's pup was one of the litter photographed on the preceding page. They all looked alike and I'm sure she would have loved any one of them, but her parents picked her pup by using the tests shown on the next page. Her dog will be easy to train.

FOLLOWING is the first test. The pup is set down and the handler walks away. Some pups will jog along underfoot and others will hold back as this pup is doing. Some won't follow at all. This pup would be scored in the middle. That's good.

COMING is next. The pup is set down and the handler steps away and kneels down calling the pup. Some pups come very fast and others are slow. This one decided that he wanted no part of the game and ran off, scared and shy. That's not good.

THE PUPPY TEST . . . THE ONE FOR YOU

This test is run when the pups are five to six weeks old. Each pup will respond differently. A score is given for each test. The easiest pup to train will be the one that is not the boldest or the shyest.

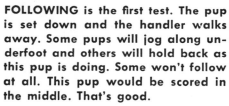

STROKING for 30 seconds shows the pup's social behavior. Some will get up and walk away and others will lie there and enjoy it. The ones that roll over and growl or bite are too bold.

RESTRAINING by holding him down will show how much he will take from humans. Some pups fight hard and struggle, others will just lie there. We want a pup to fight a little.

IRRITATING the pup by holding him off the ground will show how he will accept your domination in the training situation. Some pups snarl and try to bite and kick. A little struggle is good.

When to Start
the Training

When to start the training of a pup is where most people make their mistake. There is a lot of wrong information around about this. People mix up the dog's age and size with his ability to learn. For example: the age of a dog has been compared to the age of a child this way. A one-year-old dog is like a seven-year-old kid. A two-year-old dog is like a fourteen-year-old teen-ager, and a three-year-old dog is like a young man. A dog seven years old is like a man who is forty-nine years old, and a ten-year-old dog is like an old man. A child starts to school at age six. A lot of people think a dog should not be started in his training until he is almost a year old, which compares to the six-year-old child. Scientists have found this information wrong. They have learned that a pup five weeks old is ready to learn. When the dog is twelve weeks old, his brain is fully grown. It takes a child's brain much longer. The dog learns faster, and remember that he learns best between the ages of seven weeks and sixteen weeks. His training must start during that time.

There is another thing scientists have taught us about young dogs. A pup makes a closer and stronger friendship with his master between the seventh and twelfth weeks than at any time later in his life. They call this a bond. The strongest bond between dog and man is made during those few weeks. That is the time training should start. There are other things that are important to know. A pup should not be taken from its mother until he is seven weeks old, when he is strong enough to leave her. Scientists have found it is important that the dog leave his littermates at the seventh week. For one thing, he is ready to learn and he's not going to learn from them the things you want him to know. Another thing that scientists have discovered is that the longer the pup stays with his brothers and sisters after the seventh week, the harder it is going to be to train him. The pecking order of the litter helps the pup in the first few weeks. It does damage after the seventh week. Pups who have only lived with their littermates and their mother for their first thirteen weeks, with no contact with people, cannot be trained later as working dogs. Pups who have lived only in their litter without people around for sixteen weeks cannot be trained at all. Scientists have proven this. Now you can see how important this early period is. A pup taken home to your house and trained at seven weeks of age will learn his simple commands by the time he is twelve weeks old. Being with people at this early age is an important part of his schooling. Lessons will begin when he is eight weeks old.

Bringing the Pup Home

Bringing a puppy home from the kennel is not very different from bringing a newborn sister or brother home from the hospital. All sorts of arrangements have to be made ahead of time. This is a big new experience for the pup and it is important that it be done calmly. The neighborhood kids should not be invited over yet, and there shouldn't be any yelling and jumping about with delight. Don't scare the pup. Let the pup get used to the place and be the one to show the excitement.

The first thing that the family has to decide is where the new arrival is going to live. The pup should not have the full run of the house until he is older and housebroken. The best room for him to stay in at first is the kitchen. A gate or board should be put across the doorways. In the kennel the pup lived with his brothers and sisters, and living was rather simple. It should be the same in his new home.

We want the pup to feel welcome and secure. That's why the kitchen is the best room. The kitchen is the room where most of the activity of the house takes place. It's good; the pup will not get lonely there. For the first seven weeks of his life he had his mother and littermates to play with. He will have a hard time if he is shut off by himself with the doors closed. Some people start a pup off in the bathroom. This is not a good idea. The tile floor is too cold.

The pup will be happy in the kitchen with all those good food smells and all the people around. Before the pup comes to his new home the room should be ready. Five or six layers of newspapers should be spread out to cover the whole floor. A water dish should ready for him. If he is a little upset from the trip home, he will want water right away. The pup's bed should be ready. The bed should be in a corner. A dog likes a cave-like place for sleeping. It's a hangover from the days when he lived with Uncle Stony in the cave. Even a pup will like a place where he cannot be approached from behind, and when he is in his bed he likes to see what is going on in the room. A box with one side cut out and an old blanket or pad in it will make a fine bed. Make sure the corner you pick will not be in a draft. A pup can stand the cold but not a draft.

A pup will learn where his bed is very quickly. He is going to use it a lot the first few months while he is growing. When he goes to his bed during the day, it means he is tired. He should be left alone. Do not wake him to play with him. The first few days in the new home are very important for the pup. Let him learn and feel his way. He'll like you better if you do.

Playing with the Pup

No horseplay. You will have plenty of time later to rough-house with him. The first week in the new home is very important. During this time you are really getting him ready to start his schooling. Play lessons, where he will learn in a fun way all the basic commands, will start after he is home with you about a week. Getting him ready for that is just a matter of getting him to like you.

It's fine to pick him up when you play. You have to be careful how you do it. Both hands have to be used. One hand will go under his chest and around over his front shoulder, and the other one goes under his rear end. That will give him all the support he will need, then he will not get hurt. Do not pick him up by his belly or drag him by a leg. Don't tease a pup. It may be fun to hear him bark or growl, but it's not fun for him. When he is bigger he could get even with you for that kind of treatment.

Food time is not play time, and sleep time is not play time. There are many times when you do not want to play, and it is no different with a puppy. You will be able to tell when he wants to play. A good game to play with a young pup is rolling a ball for him to chase. Even at this early age you can start to teach the command FETCH. If you say that one word, FETCH, as you roll the ball he will start to learn that sound and what that sound means. That's how he is going to learn all his commands later, by learning what the one word means and what you want him to do when you say it.

Pups like to play by themselves when there is no one else to play with. They should have their own toys. A bone is fine. Be sure it's a shinbone and will not splinter. If he swallowed a sharp bone, it could hurt him. A ball is a good toy. The ball must be hard enough so he cannot chew pieces out of it. If he eats a large piece of a ball, it could kill him. Rawhide chewies are good. Do not give him an old shoe. If he gets to like chewing on shoes, someday he may find a good one and not know the difference. Mom won't like it if he destroys a good shoe.

Puppies like to play tug of war with straps and things. Don't do it. It only teaches him how strong his teeth are and he might become a chewer. Short periods of romping with him as he did with his littermates are good, but remember he's just a baby, so go easy and let him win the game of romp. Roll him over. Let him get up. Let him climb all over you. He should not get too excited. If he does, stop and hold him in your arms and talk to him. Stroking him will calm him down. He'll like that.

FETCH. Roll the ball and he'll learn that fast.

When It's Time for Bed

A new pup brought into the house is going to be alone for the first time when he is put to bed that night. He has always had his brothers and sisters to sleep with. Now he is by himself in the kitchen. The house is quiet. You have gone to bed. It is not easy for the young dog. He wants to be with you. He'll start to bark and even howl. That's his way of calling you. He has to learn to be alone, that this is the way it is going to be. He'll keep the family awake for a while, then he'll get tired and settle down to sleep. It is important that you do not go to the kitchen and try to make him stop barking. That would only teach him that when he barks you will come to him. That will only make him bark more. The first night he may bark a lot. The second night he will try again to call you. He will not bark as much. By the third night he'll have learned that barking will not do him any good, so he might as well sleep. You can see, he's already starting to learn.

Bedtime can be any time of the day for a young growing pup. Let him get his rest. All babies need a lot of sleep because they are growing so fast. He'll want to play when he wakes up; be kind and let him sleep.

Pups Shouldn't Always Get Their Way

We have seen that the pup learned that howling at night wasn't going to bring you to the kitchen in the middle of the night. The lesson he learned was that he didn't get his way. Just as you know that you do not always get your way at home or in school, the dog has to learn it too. He has to learn to put up with things he does not like. For example: sometime during that first week you should put a collar on him. For the first few days he should have it on for only a few hours. He will not like it and it will bother him. He'll scratch at it and try to get it off. In a short time he'll learn to live with it. Once he's used to the collar, a leash should be attached to it. For a short period each day he should drag it around the floor while he's living in the kitchen. It will not take him long to get used to it. There will be times when Mother is in the kitchen trying to cook and the pup, underfoot, is in the way. The leash should be tied to a doorknob or something that will keep the dog out of the way. He'll put up a fuss at the end of the leash. He'll learn that he might as well lie down and put up with the restriction. He'll also learn that the leash means control. He cannot get away when it is on. This will be important later. It's little things like this that set the stage for his learning.

It is unfair to the dog not to teach him from the very beginning what he can do and what he cannot do. If you think about this for a minute, you'll agree that neither kids nor dogs should always do only the things they like. Kids that do only what they want become spoiled brats . . . pups are no different. If you don't try new things that might even be difficult at first, you'll never know if you'll like them.

he leash and collar are not much fun but he learns to put up with them.

Restrained by the leash tied to the desk to keep him out of the way, Beau is . . .

Beau wants to play and gets a little rough with the cat. She wants none of that . . .

. . greeted by a friend who has all the freedom in the world. They nuzzle and kiss.

. . so off she goes. Now what does he do? He has learned the leash means stay put.

Even Gretchen feels bad that Tar has to be scolded. If he is reprimanded right away he will learn not to use the living room as his bathroom. Be firm but kind.

Housebreaking

One of the reasons not to give the pup the full run of the house when you bring him home at the age of seven weeks is that he cannot be housebroken at that early age. It takes a child a few years to be toilet-trained. It takes a pup only a few weeks to have control and to learn that he must go outside.

To start, the pup is living in the one room and the floor is covered with about five layers of papers. Usually a pup will go to the far corner of the room, away from his bed, to do his business. The soiled papers should be picked up as soon as possible. The underneath papers that are not soiled should not be removed. Clean papers should be put down on top of them. Next time he goes the scent will attract him to that spot again. If by error he soils the papers close to his bed or not in the far corner, pick up all the papers in that area. We want him to learn to use the papers and to use them in one area. He'll catch onto this very fast. In a week or so you will see that the papers in the other area can be taken up. The area he should use can gradually be made smaller and smaller. Then he will be paper-trained.

Some people always like to have the dog paper-trained so that if they must be away from the house a long time the dog can take care of his needs himself. Others use the paper training to teach the dog that when they go for a walk the dog is expected to relieve himself at that time. To do that, some of the lower layers of the paper on the floor are taken to the street. The pup is taught to be curbed by placing the papers down for him to sniff. Soon he will get the idea that when he is walked he is supposed to do his business. Any time the pup does the right thing he should be praised.

A young pup usually has to go right after he has eaten. If he is put outside or taken out immediately, he'll soon learn that doing his business outside is even better for him. He'll like it better and will be smart enough to learn to scratch on the door to signal that he wants to go out. This will happen when he is four or five months old. The paper is the best way to start because at such a young age he doesn't have much control. Accidents will happen. That's what the paper is for. If you live in a house with a back yard, both ways can be used at the same time. The paper on the floor will take care of the accidents, and taking the pup out after meals will show him what you want. When you do walk the pup outside, do not rush him. As soon as he is finished, praise him and take him right back inside. He'll then get the idea that you want him to go outside to relieve himself.

Once the pup has learned to go outside and to use the paper inside, he can be given more of a run of the house. You are going to have to watch him closely.

The Commands...
First One Is No

I'll bet that if there is one thing you wish your folks never said to you it would be "No." Wouldn't that be fun? Think of all the trouble you could get into. Or, would it be fun? If your baby sister started to walk off the curb into the street you, too, would say, "No!" No, even if we don't like it, is a very important word. It teaches us right from wrong and what is expected of us.

If the young pup has an accident and wets in the house, the command will, of course, be NO. When you give the command, make sure you use a stern voice. He will then know that you are not happy about what he has done. Do not be too rough, but make sure he knows you are not pleased. To use the command NO, you must use it only at the time you catch him doing the wrong thing. There is the big difference between training a kid and training a dog. If a kid does something wrong and it is not discovered until sometime later, he can still be punished for it. Not so with the dog. If his wrong act is discovered only five minutes later and you punish him, he will not know why he is being punished. A teacher can explain to a pupil what he has done wrong. A trainer cannot explain to a dog something that he has done wrong in the past. There is no reasoning with a dog. In order to train the dog to the command NO, he has to be caught in the act of doing something wrong.

What would you do if you came home and found that your dog had chewed up a book while you were gone? You could not punish the pup. Next time put the book away. That's what your mother has been telling you to do all along.

Eric wanted to read but Beau wanted to play. The pup had to learn NO.

ic commanded NO. Beau was not sure so he howled his objection. He wanted to . . .

ay. The command was repeated and Beau got the point. He lay down and waited.

One way a dog learns is by putting him into a situation and having him learn that it won't hurt him. Here Eric is teaching him that this will be his place when they travel by car. He gets used to it and learns to love it. The other way a dog learns is by direct command. You have just seen Eric give Beau the NO command. Beau learns his place while in the car, but there is no command for it.

Different Ways a Pup Learns

A young pup learns things two ways. The first way is by figuring out the answer to things himself. The second way he learns is by being taught things he has to know. Here is an example of each way of learning. A very young pup has to learn that riding in a car is not anything to be afraid of, in fact it can be fun. At first the motion seems strange. He'll get very quiet and seem uneasy on his first ride because he doesn't know what is happening. By the time he has taken his second or third trip there is no problem whatsoever. He has learned all by himself that the car noises won't hurt him. The motion is fun and so is going someplace with the family. The pup learns to like the car. The NO command, which we have just read about, is the other way of learning. He has to be taught things that he cannot learn himself, just as you are taught in school.

Scientists have discovered some very important information about both ways the puppy learns. First, the learning the pup does himself has an important effect on the training he will receive from his master. They have also found that a puppy must learn all the self-taught things at a very early age. That is why we start the pup at seven weeks. The first two weeks of the training are learning the world around him. If the self-learning starts later, the pup will have fears. Those fears hinder the learning the pup receives from his trainer. Teaching the command NO to a dog that has fears is very difficult.

It is very important in the training that the pup receive as many experiences of life at a very early age. He should be taken on walks. He should be taken downtown. He should meet strangers. He should do all the things he will do later. Without even knowing it, he'll learn to like everything. Now the pup is about to learn the simple commands. We will teach them to him the same way he learned that the car was fun. We will show him what we want, but there will be no reprimand with the learning.

We will call this kindergarten play lessons. These play lessons are given when the pup is between the age of nine weeks and twelve weeks. He'll learn SIT, STAY, COME, but remember you cannot scold him if he does things wrong at this age.

Gretchen tried to teach Tar the command KENNEL. He didn't get the idea and lay down. He just didn't understand what she wanted.

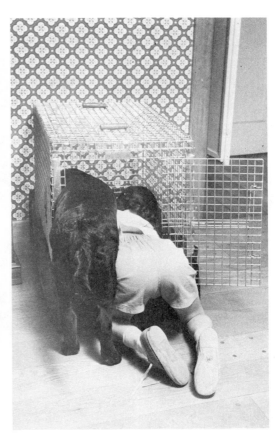

...retchen taught her pup the KENNEL command by playing a game with the ...nnel-Aire in the house. She gave the command and they both tried it. She ...on. He learned.

...e Kennel-Aire is a fine "private room" for a dog at home, while camping or ...the car. Even Uncle Stony's dogs loved a cave. It makes them feel secure.

A dog should get all kinds of experiences at a very early age so that he will have no fear of new things. He has to learn to deal with people, other dogs, and strange objects and places. A dog that learns this early will be secure. He'll be easier to train if he is happy and not afraid.

The Training Collar

The training collar can be made of either leather or metal chain. It's called a choke collar, but that is a bad name for it. It can choke, but it's not supposed to be used that way. It will have two large rings, one at each end. There is a right and wrong way to put it on. The pictures show how to do it correctly. The loop goes over the dog's head and the leash is attached to it. When you want to correct the dog for doing something wrong, a sharp pull on the leash will tighten the collar. Don't pull and hold the collar tight. A quick jerk is all that is needed. Then the collar will release quickly without causing any pain.

Don't be rough on the dog if he is not paying attention to his lessons. Be sure you treat the dog the way you would like to be treated by your parents and teachers. Some people run after their dog with a rolled-up newspaper and swat at him and shout. That will never do. The dog can run faster and get away. The rolled-up newspaper only teaches the dog to hate newspaper delivery boys. You will find that this collar will mean control to the dog. He does not like the collar tightened around his neck any more than you like a spanking. After he learns what the collar can do, just jiggling it will get him back to his lessons.

Put the choke collar on the dog only when you are training him or walking and working him. It's possible for the collar to catch on a branch or something and trap the dog.

ere is the whole collar with a ring at each end. Slip the chain through one ring.

et it drop and make a loop, then open the loop up and spread it apart. Slip the . . .
. . . loop over the pup's head. Turn the chain around; hook the leash to it.

The Kindergarten Lessons

When the pup is about nine weeks old and has learned all about the house and the people in it, he will be ready to learn his commands. Schooling now begins. To go to school, the pup has to wear his collar and his leash. Both the leash and the collar should be very lightweight. The leash should be about six feet long. The collar and leash will come to mean control to the pup. He'll have to do what is expected of him. He won't be able to get away.

The lessons will be very short. Five or ten minutes will be enough. You can do the lessons three times a day. You will be surprised how fast he will learn.

The classroom should be in a quiet place. A lawn is good, or a big room. The two of you should be alone. No other children or other animals should be around. You will want to have the pup's complete attention.

The plan will be to teach command SIT first. After he learns that, you will teach command STAY, and the last command will be COME. Let me explain why they should be taught in that order. If you have the pup on a leash and you start to teach COME, how are you going to get away from the dog so that he can come to you? If you teach SIT, then

STAY, you can then move away from him to teach him to come to you on command COME.

Remember, you are the teacher and there is no reprimand during the kindergarten lessons. We want the pup to like these games. If he does not get the idea of a command, don't scold him, just start over with him. We will show you how to do it.

Plan to do the training when he is not sleepy, and do not do it just after he has eaten. Don't romp and play with the pup just before you start the lessons.

Scratch, scratch, scratch. At first he'll think it's terrible but the leash and collar are his school clothes. He'll get used to them. The leash and collar are important for teaching all commands.

After Kindergarten
...to School

Adults are astonished that a pup in kindergarten will actually learn the SIT, STAY, COME commands at such an early age. Of course, at that early age he can't be depended upon to do them just right each time. At the end of kindergarten he's only twelve weeks old. Scientists have discovered that between twelve and sixteen weeks of age a pup continues to learn at a very rapid rate and that this is the time for a dog to learn disciplined behavior. At this age he should be made to do the simple SIT, STAY, COME commands. This is the time when it is decided who is going to be the boss, you or the dog. Scientists have found that a pup at age seventeen weeks starts to show his independence. The pup will then act like a teen-ager who is testing his parents to see how much he can get away with. If a pup does not receive his schooling before that, chances are he'll be a spoiled brat all his life.

Schooling is only a continuation of the kindergarten lessons. The only difference will be that now the pup will have to do his lessons and he'll have to do them correctly. In the pictures we will show both the kindergarten lessons with the younger puppy, and the in-school lessons with the older pup. Michele, with her black Labrador, whom she named Mac, will be showing how to handle the pup in kindergarten. Mac was between eight and nine weeks old when these pictures were taken. Michele's brother, Eric, will be showing what his dog Waldo, a springer spaniel, must learn in school. Waldo was only thirteen weeks old when these pictures were taken.

Most of the discipline after the kindergarten period can be done with the tone of your voice. A sharply spoken NO . . . NO! will show a pup that you are not pleased with what he is doing. It will straighten him out. Reprimand does not have to be cruel or harsh.

You have to make sure a pup does what is expected of him. If you command SIT and he is not sure he wants to do it, instead of just pushing his hindquarters down, give it a wack with your hand. Command SIT in a stern voice. He'll sit. Quickly change your voice back to a pleasant tone and say, "That's a good fellow." Give him a pat.

Between the twelfth and sixteenth weeks you can gradually lengthen the time on the STAY command. He should be able to sit waiting for the COME command for as much as two minutes. If he starts to get up to come to you before the command is given, jump at him. Shout, "SIT! STAY." He'll do it.

You should always end the lesson with the pup doing the right thing. Then you can praise him and he will like it when you start the class the next time. As you know from your own schooling, there are days when things do not go well. If you see that your pup is having one of those bad days, cut the class short. For example: if the pup can't seem to stay seated on the STAY command, but wants to come to you, quickly command COME as he goes to get up. Then he has done the correct thing. Now you can end the class on a happy note. Good teachers know they do not always get their way. In teaching, be firm but fair and give lots of praise.

When you think the pup understands the STAY command,

Eric was teaching Beau the command SIT. Beau was getting tired and decided to COME instead of SIT. Eric saw he was tired and quickly said COME. Now the dog was doing the right thing and Eric could stop the training on a happy note. He could praise the pup and the dog wouldn't mind starting the class the next time.

there is a next step to take. Have the pup SIT, STAY. Then you drop the leash and slowly step backward. As you go back, repeat the STAY command and give the traffic cop's hand signal to stop. Then duck out of sight around a corner. Wait only a second. Pop back in view. If he has moved, start all over. If he has not moved, command STAY again. Drop out of sight for another second. Come back and command COME. Give him lots and lots of praise. That's very good for a very young pup, but he can do this with no trouble. Each day lengthen the time you are out of sight. If you are doing this lesson outside, by time the pup is sixteen weeks old you should be able to run all the way around the house while he waits for you. You can surprise him from the other direction.

The leash and collar are part of the pup's school dress. All lessons should be done using them. He gets to know that they mean control. When you are sure he knows the commands, you can start to give them without using the leash. When you are not holding class, spring the commands on him. Try him on SIT and STAY while you are preparing his supper. Try it when you are both just playing. Do it only a few times a day. Do not nag the pup with his lessons. You know from school that a student gets tired of too much teaching.

This is the time when you can speak firmly to a pup. The command NO has to be understood. If he makes a mistake about his housebreaking, let him know that you are unhappy. If he chews on the leg of a chair instead of his toys, let him know about it.

We have been telling you all along that the pup should be started in his training at this early age. If for some reason the dog is older, and you did not get your pup when we have told you to, these training methods should still be used. It's going to mean that the training is going to be more difficult with an older dog. You'll be using the NO command a lot.

Michele started to teach her pup, age 9 weeks, to walk on the leash. At first she tried pulling him along. He just sat down, not knowing what was expected.

Walking on Leash

All the lessons are going to be learned with the leash on. The pup has to learn how to walk with you on lead. He was wearing the collar and dragging the leash around the house during those first weeks. That was a little uncomfortable for him, but now that we are going to use the leash, the pup is used to the idea of having it on.

The dog should learn from the beginning to walk on your left side if you are a right-handed person. This custom got started back in Uncle Stony's time. He taught his dogs to walk or HEEL on his left. He carried a big club in his right hand on his walks. The dog was taught to be on the left so he would be out of the way of the club. If you are walking with your dog and carrying a package, it will be better for you if you have the dog on the left. Left-handed trainers have their dogs walking on the right side.

he stopped and waited. She talked quietly to him. He fought the leash and collar.

His leash held short, he finally got into position and walked off nicely.

Eric shows what Beau can do at only 16 weeks of age. See how he holds the leash

In order to walk with the pup, the leash should be held short in your left hand. The excess length should be coiled and held in the right hand. That will place the dog very close to your left knee. That is where he should always be.

When you start walking with the pup, he might balk and try to pull away. Don't yank him. Be gentle. Coax him to try walking with you. Pat him and show him that you are really friends. Call him by name and start again. When he gets the idea and comes along, praise him. Stop and tell him what a good fellow he is. He'll like that.

Later we will teach him how to heel with you. To start, we just want him to walk along. You will have to be the one who keeps him on the left. If he crosses over in front of you, you should move so that he is back on your left side. If he is always on your left side, he will come to know that is where you want him to be.

Do not expect too much from the pup at this age. He'll learn to HEEL later. For now, all we want is for him not to object to being on the leash. Even if he does not walk with you too well at this point, he is ready to learn the first command, SIT.

au starts out slowly but he's enjoying the walk. Hold the dog's
ad up. Walk at his pace. Encourage him so he'll learn his place.

The Commands...
The Words

Let me ask you a question. If a new kid moved into your neighborhood and he did not speak English, how would you talk to him? I'm sure that before you learned his language or he learned yours, you would use your hands to get ideas across to him. For example, if you wanted to tell him to sit, you could figure out how to do it. You could point to a chair. If he still did not get the idea, you could walk him to the chair and put your hand on his shoulder and gently push him down. If you wanted him to stay, you could show him by putting out the palms of your hands, toward him. If you wanted him to come, you would wave your hand in a coming motion and he'd get the idea. We do a lot of talking to each other with the motions of our bodies.

The traffic cop, without saying a word, can stop the cars by putting up his hand. Your teacher can stop you talking in class by just pointing at you and giving you a look. When two boys are about to have a fight, their bodies signal their anger. The smaller of the two will stand up straighter. The boy who is more aggressive will push his head forward. You can meet a kid on the street and you can tell as he walks up, before he says a word, if he is friendly. Dogs are even better than we are at reading these signs.

Back in the time when his language was very simple, Old Uncle Stony was an expert at reading sign language. He used his ears, nose, and eyes to learn. Today we depend mostly on words to do our learning. Our senses of hearing and smell are not as good as they once were because we have stopped using them. Dogs have not lost their senses. They still learn all the signs just as when they were in the wild.

To teach a dog, you will have to use sign language along with your voice to show the dog what the words mean. The young pup is not very different from the kid who moved into your neighborhood and could not speak English. How would you teach a pup what the word SIT meant? You would say SIT and at the same time gently push the pup into a sitting position. He can't miss what the word means. We'll show you how that is done and what signs to use with the other commands.

THE COMMAND IS . . . SIT

Here is the way we teach the command SIT. You will be walking with the pup on the leash. When you are about to give the command to sit, you will take the leash in your right hand. The command will be FIDO, SIT. As you speak, pull his head up with the leash that's in your right hand. At the same time use your left hand to push down on his hindquarters. Hold his head up and his rear down for only a second and repeat the command SIT. Then release him and give him a lot of praise. Tell him he's a good fellow and pat him. The first few times you try it you may have to use a lot of pressure to make him sit. Then you will see that he will sit with less and less hand pressure each time you try it. In only a few lessons you will find that you only have to touch his hindquarters with your fingers. Your hand will only have to remind him that the command means sit. In a few days you will see that you will not have to use the left hand at all. Give the command FIDO, SIT, pull up on his head, and he'll sit.

SIT is the control command. It's the same as when your teacher calls on you in class. When she calls your name, you sit up and wait for her question. SIT puts the pup under control. Now he is ready for the next command.

Michele teaches Black to sit. They are both learning. He'll do it on command in a few days. On the next page Eric shows how he trained his dog to sit. At 16 weeks of age he'll do it on voice command, off the leash.

Standing next to the pup, Eric holds his head up with the leash. He commands SIT and touches Beau's rear end to remind him what he wants him to do. In the lower pictures he applies more pressure until the dog gets the idea that SIT means to lower the back end! He keeps the pup's head up.

Even in kindergarten, Michele's pup Black learns to stay. On the next page, Beau, who is in school, shows how it is done. At 16 weeks of age he can do this off-lead.

THE COMMAND IS . . . STAY

We teach the pup to stay while he is in the sitting position. The command STAY will mean to stay seated. Here is the way it is done.

First you will command SIT. The pup now knows this. He will sit. Then you command STAY. On giving the new command, you step in front of the dog, facing him. Hold the palm of your hand in front of his face. Repeat the command STAY. You are holding your hand as the traffic policeman does when he halts the cars . . . palm out, facing the dog. That is the hand sign to show the dog what the command word means. Repeat the command and the hand sign. We hope that he will stay seated. If not, go back and stand next to him and command SIT. Then repeat the STAY command and step in front of him, giving the hand signal at the same time. If he stays for only a few seconds, tell him how good he is. Praise him. Give him a hug. Pat him. Make him know he was a good fellow. Do this two or three times and stop. That's an excellent first lesson.

Later the same day or the next day do it again. This time when he holds the sit, take a step backward. Give the pup the

Command SIT. Walk in front of dog; change leash to left hand.

Command STAY. Use the traffic cop's signal. Walk around, he'll stay.

policeman's signal to stop. Command STAY and step back again. Do not make the pup hold the stay too long. A few seconds will do. Each time you take a step back let the leash out.

Remember, he is only a baby. He will not be perfect. Most people who have a dog would not believe that a pup so young

1.

Beau is ready for advanced work. In picture 1 he is commanded to SIT, STAY. The command STAY is repeated and slowly Eric walks backwards. He keeps showing the traffic cop's signal as he goes. In picture 2 he gets to the end of the leash. In picture 3 he drops it. Now the dog has his freedom if he wishes to run off. He won't. Eric takes a step back in picture 4. Beau holds. The trick here is to make all steps and movements slowly. Quick, jerky movements will have the pup up and coming to you. The big test comes on the next page.

can do this. If you are kind and gentle with him at this age of about ten weeks, he'll do these commands. If he is not pushed too hard, he will like doing it. If he does, the next command, COME, is going to be very easy for him.

2.

3.

4.

THE COMMAND IS . . .
STAY

1. Command SIT, STAY. Drop the leash.

2. Step back but continue giving the command STAY with the hand signal.

3. Hide behind the corner of the building for only a second or so.

Step out so he can see you and give the commands. If he doesn't stay . . .

. . . start all over from the beginning. Beau stayed, so Eric hid again.

Hide longer each time. He'll learn to hold command STAY a long time.

At only 9 weeks Black has learned to stay. Michele has learned to do the . . .

THE COMMAND IS . . . COME

You can now put the three commands together. First the control command, SIT. The STAY command is next. You will have moved back six feet to the end of the leash on the STAY command. Now, to teach COME is easy. You are in a standing position with your hand out in the traffic cop position. Kneel down, squat, and at the same time command COME. He'll get up and bound for you. That's the time to give him a big hug and pat him. Make a fuss over him. He'll love it. Kneeling down to his level is a friendly signal to a dog. That's why he'll come to you so easily.

If, for some reason, he is not sure what you want on this command, there is an easy way to show him. When you squat down at the end of the leash and call COME, give the leash a gentle tug. He'll get the idea of what that signal means.

That is all we are going to teach the pup in kindergarten.

. . job just like Eric. See her stance? The trick to make the dog come . . .

. . . is easy. All Michele has to do is drop to her knees and command COME. Getting down on the ground is a friendly gesture to the dog, so he'll come a-running. It's that easy.

Eric shows one of the class lessons that he and Beau do every day.

THE COMMAND IS . . . COME

We got the pup ready for these lessons between the seventh and ninth weeks. We started him in kindergarten and during the next three weeks he learned what the three commands mean. The most important thing is that he is learning to learn. If you are kind to him and he likes this learning, he will want to learn and please you the rest of his life.

In these early lessons the hand signals are important. They are the things that teach the pup the meaning of the voice commands.

f course when Eric drops to the ground the pup will come to him.

They do this off of the leash. He tests the pup by doing the STAY and COME commands around the house. When in class the leash is on.

1.

2.

THE COMMAND IS . . . COME

Eric shows how to train a dog that does not understand what is meant by the command COME. Picture 1 is the STAY position. Then he drops to his knees in picture 2. When he commanded COME the pup did not do so. In picture 3 Eric got up and ran away from the dog and kept shouting COME. The dog wanted to be with him, so he followed. Off they ran, picture 4. When the pup caught up to him, down on the ground they both went. Eric told his pup what a good boy he was. The next time they played COME the pup obeyed because he did want to be close to his master.

4.

Eric told his pup what a good boy he was.

Some Review and Some Progress

Each day the pup will get a better idea of what is expected. The lessons will always start the same way. Walk with the dog at your side with the leash held short. As he learns the command SIT, you will not have to lean over and push his rear end down. If he does not do it right away, touching his back with your finger will be enough to remind him what is expected. Even that will not be necessary after a few weeks. Lifting his head with the leash will also remind him that the command SIT means: do it now.

Through this period of schooling command STAY has gradually been extended. The pup should sit and stay until released. The hand signal of the policeman should always remind the dog what the word stay means. When you go to the store to do an errand, tie the leash to a post on the street. Give the command STAY and go into the store and do your errand. The pup has to learn that he has to wait. If he makes a fuss, let him bark. He'll learn that it does no good. Don't scold him if he's still barking when you come back to him. Next time make the waiting period longer. He'll get tired of barking. When he is quiet when you return, then praise him.

The COME command was started on the leash. You moved to the end of the leash to give the command. To remind him what the command meant, you tugged on the leash and if necessary drew him in. A dog does some things for very interesting reasons. Did you ever see a dog go to the corner of a room and circle around then lie down to sleep? He learned that habit back in the days when he lived in the cave with old Uncle Stony. The dog went to the corner because he felt safe there. With his back to the wall, his enemies could approach from only one direction. He circled before he lay down so he could see if the area was safe. That is the way a dog protects himself. He has a way of protecting himself on the COME command. A dog does not like to have another animal, man included, towering over him. He notices things like that. If you want the dog to come to you, show him that you are a friend. Bend over when you call him.

The COME command is learned on the leash, but you will use it when he is off the leash. If he does not seem to want to obey while he has the freedom of being off the leash, try this trick. Have him SIT, STAY. You move away from him. If, when you call him, he does not come, even when you squat down to show him that you are his friend, then turn and run away from him. As you run, clap your hands and call his name. He'll want to be with you, so he'll come bounding to you. Praise him.

I had a hunting dog once that would not come when he was off the leash. I soon cured him of that. He ran off and I called him, but he paid no attention to me. I let him go. I found a heavily concealed place to hide in the woods. After a short while the dog started to wonder where I was, he then started hunting for me. I could see that he began to worry that maybe he was lost. Oh, what about all that good food and the warm bed and the nice people? He searched frantically. He finally found me and he never ran off again. He learned what the word COME meant.

New Commands...

DOWN

How would you show a dog what the command DOWN means? Put him in a lying-down position and command DOWN. Here is the way to do it. First, have the pup sit. That's the control position. Command DOWN, you squat down in front of him and pull his front paws forward . . . now he's down. Repeat the command and use a hand signal to show him what you mean. The hand signal for DOWN is the flat hand, palm out, and move the hand toward the ground as you give the command.

With a young pup this method is very easy. Lifting the front paws is not a difficult job. It's much more difficult with a large dog. In order to teach DOWN to a medium-sized dog, it might be necessary to use the choke collar and pull him down to the floor. With a big strong dog, slip the leash under your foot and pull up easily on the leash. This forces him down. You should repeat the command DOWN as you do this. Once he's down, give him a lot of praise.

Many people never train their dog to lie down. They consider a dog that will sit on command as a well-mannered, good citizen. They feel that if he wants to lie down, it is up to the dog. This command can wait until the dog is older. I agree that a dog that sits and stays is well enough trained. It's useful to keep a dog from bothering people. A seated dog can still move around enough to get in the way. It's not a hard command to teach and, as with the other commands, he has to be shown what the word "down" means.

ief teaches Ben the command DOWN. But Ben does not understand the word,
 he is shown what it means. From the sitting position Ben's front legs are
ntly lifted and pulled forward. Now he's down. While this is being done Lief
 mmands DOWN.

Lief repeats the command DOWN and shows the dog the hand
signal that goes with the voice. The hand is raised high over his
head and then brought down low, as it is in the picture. That arm
and hand motion means down and the dog will learn to do the
command on the hand signal without the voice command.

QUIET! QUIET! The left hand around the muzzle firmly shows the pup what the command means. It is not necessary to be rough. Gentle pressure is enough.

QUIET

A noisy dog, like a noisy child, is something we can all do without. If you live in an apartment, a yapping dog can drive the neighbors crazy. It's not much better on a farm. Only the other night I was staying on a farm in Virginia and they had a dog that bayed at the moon all night. It was a sleepless night until the farmer got up and shouted, "QUIET" out the window. The dog decided he needed some sleep too.

How do you get the point across to a dog that the command QUIET means to keep his mouth shut? Put your hand around his snout and hold his mouth closed. At the same time give the one-word command QUIET. If he does not seem to get the point, next time a little pressure on the snout will make him understand. Use a stern voice to make him know that you mean business. With one hand around his snout, use the other hand and shake your finger at him. It'll take only a few days and he'll stop barking on the voice command alone.

HEEL

I had a friend who was training his dog and I noticed that the back of his left sneaker was all chewed away. When I asked him about this, he answered, laughing, "I'm training my dog to heel. He's learning the command by taste!"

In the early lessons you used the leash and the collar to show the dog that you had control. He could not run away to get out of his lessons. When we started we didn't mind much how well he walked on the leash. Getting used to it was the first step. Starting at about age sixteen weeks, we will want him to learn that he has his place while walking with you. There is nothing worse than a dog who wants to lag behind and smell everything on the pavement while he's out for a walk. The pup that pulls ahead and wants to be the leader of the band is just as bad. A dog that gets in the way of other people walking is not a very good citizen. A dog has to learn his place. His place is walking next to you with his head at about your knee. Always have him walk on the correct side of you. Remember, if you are right-handed it's best to have him on the left. Never let him on the wrong side. He'll learn to come to the correct side even when he is off leash and you command HEEL.

The choke collar should be used for this training. The leash must be held short so he can't rush ahead or lag behind. If he tries to cross in front of you, bump him with your leg. He'll soon learn to stay out of your way. Each time he does something wrong, a light jerk on the choke collar and the command HEEL will show him what is expected.

Do not rush to perfect this command. It's more important that a young pup learn what is expected of him on this command than the way he performs the command. A pup is rambunctious; he'll settle down, and if he knows what to do he'll do it himself.

It's good to teach this command by voice and hand signal. The hand signal is the patting of your left leg as you say HEEL. With the leash in your right hand and slung across your knees to the dog, your left hand will be free to pat your leg. If you do this every time you give the command, shortly you will see that the dog will obey the HEEL command when you only pat your leg. You won't have to say a thing to him. Pat, pat, and he's at heel.

At heel, a dog has to learn to anticipate or know instantly what your next move is going to be. He gets this message or signal from learning to follow your left leg. Here is the way that works. With the dog on your left, command SIT. When he is seated, pat your left leg and command HEEL. Then, instantly step off walking with your left leg. If he does not respond immediately, the choke collar will tighten around his neck and jerk him. He'll soon learn to get up and start off quickly so that the nasty collar won't grab him.

The best place to teach this is on the sidewalk. When you come to the corner, even if there is no automobile traffic coming, stop. Command SIT. When you are ready to make the crossing, command HEEL; at the same time pat your leg and step off the curb with your left foot. This will teach the dog two things: to step off with you or be yanked by the leash, not to run out into the street without first stopping. This could save a pup's life.

HEEL

Beau is getting his first lesson at heeling. He's young and will not do a good job yet, but this is the time to start him. He has to learn that his place is next to your knee. The pup must always be in the same position. A short leash helps remind him where that place is. Eric forgot to pat his left leg with his hand as he commanded HEEL, but they did very well.

eau learned coming to a curb means stop, SIT. When it's safe to go, Eric commands EEL and steps forward with his left foot. Beau was not paying attention. The . . .

. . leash across Eric's left leg pulls Beau along. He'll learn to step off with Eric.

At this tender age both the pup and his mistress learn about the work ahead
in the show ring . . . work . . . fun . . . both beauties have a future.

Work Can Be Games

Back in Mr. Stone Age's time, his dogs all had jobs to do. They received pay for their work, a good supper and a warm bed. Today many of our dogs are on relief. They get their pay, room and board, and medical care for lying around all day sleeping in the boss's chair. The only job that most of them do is to wag their tails and jump around making a fuss welcoming a member of their family home. Animals, just like man, have to have work. You know how unhappy you feel when there is nothing to do? Dogs are no different. That's one reason we've trained the dog. There is also an old saying, "All work and no play makes Jack a dull boy." The training we've given the pup makes him a good citizen, but to make him happy, we have to give him something he likes to do.

We all like to play games. Dogs love it. Games make them the center of attention and they like it when you make a fuss over them and show how pleased you are. It's like your getting a gold star in school. What games can you play with your dog? There are many: FETCH, SPEAK, ROLL OVER, PLAY POSSUM, BEG, and many more. They make a pup feel important.

Don't start teaching the games until the dog has learned his basic commands. He should be ready when he's about four months old.

Oh, how Jock loves the smell of the food. Lauri will give it to him if he will make even a little sound. He really howls. Speak up . . . and he does!

SPEAK

Teaching the dog to speak is very easy. The fastest way to teach this is with food. Let the pup see that you have a little piece of food in your hand. Wave it in front of his nose. Let him smell it. Jump around and get excited. Let him see that what we are doing is fun. Command SPEAK, using a cheerful tone of voice. Try to get him so excited that he makes a sound, any sound; a bark or only a squeal will do. As soon as he makes the noise, give him the tidbit.

If he does not get the idea the first time, give him the food anyway. Try it again, but if the pup does not respond this time, do not give him the food. Try it again later. Soon he'll learn that if he wants the food he'll have to bark for it.

When he does bark on the SPEAK command, give him more than the food. Give him praise.

1. Some dogs learn to shake hands by having the undersides of their paws tapped.

2. Lauri shows another way to teach SHAKE. She lifts the right paw, pushes him . . .

3. . . . off balance. Then he gets the idea. They both enoy this game.

SHAKE HANDS

Teach command SHAKE by first having the pup SIT and
STAY. You sit and stay facing the pup. With your right
hand, reach around and tap the underside or heel of the
pup's right paw. Command SHAKE or SHAKE HANDS as
you do this. He'll take the weight off the paw that is being
touched. Pick up his right paw, shake it, command SHAKE,
and tell him how good he is. If he doesn't get the idea, try
this: as you pick up the right paw, with your left hand on
his right shoulder, push him slightly to his left. That will
throw his weight to his left side and take the weight off his
right paw. As you do this command SHAKE. It's a trick all
politicians do. Goodness, someday your dog may be elected
President. . . .

BEG

Begging is something most dogs learn on their own. A dog should not be allowed to beg except on command. It might seem cute, but it can be bothersome to people. Do not teach the dog to beg until he is strong enough to balance himself on his haunches. There are two ways to teach this game. The method you use will depend on the size of the dog. For a big dog, put him on a leash and command SIT. Stand in front of him. With your arm straight out, over his head, hold his head up with the leash. Hold a little piece of food or dog candy over his head with the other hand and command

Lauri taught Jock to sit up in a corner where his back would be supported if he lost his balance. She sat him in a corner, lifted his paws until he was upright. She held some food for him. He reached up for it and found his balance. Soon he didn't need the wall for support. This is easy to teach.

BEG. If he lifts his paw trying to get the food, give it to him. If he stands up to get the food, do not give it to him. Command SIT and start all over.

Some dogs have trouble learning to balance their bodies, but with praise they'll learn. If your pup has trouble, or if he is a small dog, you can teach this by kneeling in front of him; as he sits in front of you, lift his front paws off the ground. Put him into a position where he should be balanced on his haunches and let go. Give the command BEG as you let go. At first he may hold the position only a second or so. That's good. Give him a tidbit and praise him. He'll get the hang of it very soon.

Gretchen teaches Tar to swim to make the retrieve. Tar was bred to retrieve, so it comes naturally to him, but all breeds will do this. They get to love it. Lauri shows how to teach FETCH in the next set of pictures.

FETCH

All dogs like to play fetch. The retrievers have been bred to do this work, but all breeds can be shown how to do it. You can start a pup only a few months old playing this game. It's good while they are young to do this with a ball or an old sock stuffed with rags and knotted at the end. Don't use hard objects that will hurt their teeth. Old shoes or gloves are not good. A pup will not be able to tell the difference between an old shoe and a new one, and if he starts to retrieve one of your mother's good shoes, you'll both get into trouble. Do not use soft rubber toys, which some stores sell as dog toys. Pups can chew them apart, and if chunks of the toy are swallowed they could kill the dog. A tennis ball is fine, but I like the sock best.

Here is the way to start. Show the pup the object. Wave it in front of his nose. Jump up and down with it. If you get all excited he will too. Then throw it . . . command FETCH. When he runs for the stuffed sock, get down on your hands and knees and command COME. Coax him in to you. Tell him he's good. Use a pleasant voice and clap your hands. When he gets close enough, quickly take it from his mouth and tell him again that he's good. Pat him. Start over. Throw the sock and tell him to fetch. He may not want to give it to you, thinking that you'll take it away. If you keep throwing it after you get it, he'll learn that if he brings it to you, you'll play more.

Don't chase the pup if he refuses to bring the sock to you. That'll only teach him to run away from you. Instead, if he doesn't want to bring the sock to you, run away from him. Clap your hands, call his name, be excited, he'll come toward you . . . running. When he is near you, turn and take the sock from his mouth and tell him how good he is. Do it all again.

As the pup gets older, you can add something to the game. Once he learns that fetch is a fun game, have him do it from a position of sitting at heel. Put the leash and choke collar on him to teach this. Command HEEL, SIT. Throw the sock. Make him wait a second or so before you command FETCH. If he breaks and runs for the sock as you throw it, but before you command FETCH, the leash and choke collar will bring him up sharp. He'll learn to wait for the command.

FETCH

Lauri gets Jock excited with the fetching dummy. She jumps and prances. Oh, he . .

When he picks it up she kneels down and starts calling him and commands . . .

. wants it. She throws the dummy and he goes for it. She commands FETCH.

. COME.

CARRYING

Holding an object in his mouth, like a rolled-up leash or newspaper, is a fun job or trick for a pup. It's easy to teach. You can use the stuffed sock for teaching this. Command SIT. With your hand over the top of his snout, gently slip your fingers between his teeth. When he opens his mouth slip the sock in. Hold his mouth closed over the sock and command HOLD. Do not hold it long. He will most likely spit it out as soon as you let go. Do it again and be nice to him and tell him he's doing fine. Try this a few times a day. Once he gets the idea, you can then have him walk at heel carrying things for you. That's fun.

Open his mouth . . . rub his chest . . . command HOLD and he'll strut with pride.

Lay him on his side.

Stroke him gently. Talk softly.

Put his head down.

Stroke him. Whisper PLAY POSSUM.

PLAY POSSUM

To teach the pup to speak, you had to get all excited yourself and hoped the dog would get excited too, then bark. To
teach the command PLAY POSSUM, you have to be very
calm and quiet. Wait until the dog is settled down to teach
him this trick. Make him lie down. Gently roll him on his
side and stroke him. Quietly command PLAY POSSUM and

The **STAY** command will help if he starts to move. He won't. He likes it.

add the command STAY. He'll like this. When he feels relaxed, stop stroking him and command PLAY POSSUM again. Slowly take your hands away. Command STAY. Do not try to make him lie still too long. Release him by telling him, "Good fellow! Good fellow." Give the pup praise.

If you have trouble teaching this and he wants to get up as soon as you stop stroking him, a hand to hold him down will teach him what you want.

ROLL OVER

This trick should be taught to your dog after he has learned to play possum. Once the pup learns to lie on his side, teaching him to roll over on his back is easy. Kneel next to him and take hold of his front and back paws that are under-

1. Take hold of his front and back paws that are on the ground.

2. Lift them gently and command ROLL OVER.

neath. With one paw in each hand, roll him over on his back and let go. Command ROLL OVER as you do this. He'll then get up on his feet. Praise him and tell him how good he is. Soon he'll do this command by the flipping motion your hands make to roll him over. This becomes his hand signal to do the trick.

3. Flip him over on his back, then all the way over.

Command ROLL OVER and praise him. That shows him what you mean.

1.

JUMP THE STICK

In picture 1 Lauri commands JUMP THE STICK. She gets the dog excited and they play chase. When he is after her she goes over the stick and commands JUMP THE STICK. She has shown him what the command means. In picture 2 her mother holds the stick low. Lauri has the dog SIT and STAY. Then she calls the dog and steps back to run away. She commands JUMP THE STICK as she calls him. See picture 3. Once he does this on command and knows what you mean by the command he will do it, as in picture 4. Lauri holds the stick and gives the command.

2.

3.

4.

Bad Dog?

Dogs, just like kids, can learn some bad habits, but they weren't born with them. Somebody let them learn the wrong things. Dealing with a spoiled brat, whether it's a kid or a dog, is difficult. Suppose a child marked the walls of his home with crayon when his mother was not around. On discovering it, she would tell him in no uncertain words that she was dis-

The important thing in training is that the dog learn you mean what you say . . .

pleased and a suitable punishment would be given. We would hope the explanation from the mother and the punishment would teach the child not to do that again. It does not work that way with a dog. Let's say that a pup gets into the garbage while the family is out, and spreads it all over the house. When you get home and discover the mess, what can you do about it? Telling the dog that it was a wrong thing to do is going to be very difficult because dogs do not understand our language. You can say to a child, "That's wrong," and the child knows what that means . . . a dog doesn't. And a dog has a very short memory. A dog does not recall things as we do. When you teach a kid to do something, the second time the teacher will say, "Remember what I told you yesterday?" The child will then try to recall what the teacher said. That's the way a teacher teaches. With a dog we do it differently. We teach a dog by habit. We do the same thing over and over until the dog learns that habit. Telling the dog that getting into the garbage and even punishing him for that will not solve the problem. The next time you go out and leave the garbage so he can get at it, . . . you can be sure he'll get in it to get the food scraps.

. **Make sure the dog understands you, then make him obey or he'll become spoiled.**

As you can see, breaking a dog of bad habits would be a very difficult job. In many cases it takes a professional dog trainer to do it. The dog-training system that we have been showing you in this book eliminates the problems of the bad dog. With the help of scientists we have been showing you that starting a pup in his training at a very early age prevents bad habits from getting started.

Proof of this training method can be seen in the dogs that guide blind people on the street. The early training method which we have been showing you is the same method that is used for the dogs that guide the blind. Early training is the key to the method. A pup is taken from the litter at seven weeks of age and started in his training. Boys and girls of your age are doing the training of these future Seeing Eye dogs. Volunteers or organizations like the 4-H Club are placing pups in homes of families with children. The kids are taught exactly how to raise the pup and train him in the early commands and in good citizenship. Of course a pup can't be taught the things he has to know for leading the blind until he is full grown, big and strong enough to wear the special harness. Scientists have learned that, if you wait until the dog is big enough to do the work and then start the basic training, he has already learned too many bad habits and will not accept this most difficult kind of training. The training, as shown here in this book, is the same that the children learn to do for the future guide dog.

These dogs can't be bad dogs, do destructive things, or bother people. They can't make any mistakes. A blind person's life depends on the dog.

Proof of the pudding are the results the children get from this early training method. Before this system was used, the training of guide dogs did not start until the dog was about a year old and full grown, but only 20 per cent of the dogs from the best guide-dog breeding were able to accept this rigorous training; 80 per cent were not dependable. Scientists studying learning habits found that dogs learned fastest while still very young. They discovered that it was very important that the dog learn the right things between eight and sixteen weeks of age. They were going to learn during that time anyway, so it became necessary for them to learn the right things. That's where the children came into the picture. Scientists found out another important fact. Between the ages of seven and twelve weeks dogs make the strongest bond with man, and if that bond is not started at that time it will never be made as strong at a later time. That's why the pup should be taken from the litter at the early age. The 4-H kids do a big job. They make that first bond with the dog, and the dog learns the teacher-pupil role. They also teach the dog his early commands and see to it that he becomes a good citizen.

With that early bond made, the dog wants to please. The NO command becomes very important. If you are stern but kind with the NO command, the pup will learn what he can do and what he cannot do. The big problem most people have is that they do not give the NO command on every occasion when the young pup does something wrong. That teaches the pup that there are times when he can get away with murder. He'll keep trying and testing to see if you will give in. You know what I'm saying. Kids do it too, but they stop when they find out that they can't get away with it.

This may sound odd to you, but training a dog to be a well-mannered, obedient, and good citizen without problems is like going to the dentist every so often to have a checkup. With a routine check, the dentist can prevent the development of serious problems. He can catch the trouble before it gets bad. In many ways, that is what you have to do in the training of your dog. Bad habits shouldn't be allowed to get started.

Training a dog means that you have to take a lot of responsibility. If something goes wrong, it will most likely be your fault, not the pup's. The first and most important question you can ask yourself is: Does the dog understand what I want? The second question is: Am I being consistent with the dog? For example: if for some reason you do not want the dog to be a barker inside the house, are you always telling him NO when he barks, or are you only telling him NO when you don't want him to do it. He will learn by this not to bark when you tell him, but he won't be learning that you don't want him to bark indoors. Be consistent in the training and the pup will get the message. Be inconsistent and you will have a confused dog.

The 4-H kids do a grand job, and the rules they follow in training are simple. Make sure the dog understands what you want. Be consistent and always do things the same way. Be Johnny-on-the-spot when it comes to reprimanding the dog. Never scold a dog for a misdeed if you have not caught him in the act, or he won't know why he's being scolded. Be kind to the dog even when you scold him. Get it over with and get things back to being fun. Treat your dog the way you'd like to be treated and he won't get into bad habits.

PROOF OF THE PUDDING

Mike and his dog Oliver have a big job ahead. Mike will give the pup his early training, then when Oliver is a year old he will be sent to school to learn how to lead a blind person through life. Scientists have learned that Oliver must start his training as soon as he leaves his mother at the young age of 49 days. The early training will be Mike's job. Learning will be a way of life for Oliver because he was started so young. He will always learn to learn. Here they are both working, delivering newspapers. The hard job for Mike, a member of the 4-H Club, is to send his pup away to school, but he'll start training another dog.

Oliver must receive training every day and be reprimanded when he does wrong. He has to get many experiences of life at an early age so that he will have no fear of any situation. He rides in cars, goes downtown, meets people, to get ready to do all the things a blind person will need him to do.

A half year later Oliver is leading a blind man. A job well done.

REMEMBER WHEN THE PUP FIRST ARRIVED.

THERE WAS A LOT OF LOVE.

THERE WAS A LOT OF WORK TO DO.

THE DOG LIKED THE WORK.

IT WAS A REWARDING EXPERIENCE FOR ALL.

About the Author

Richard A. Wolters, an authority in the field of dog training, has written several books on the subject, including *Gun Dog*, *Water Dog*, *Family Dog*, and *City Dog*. He is an avid photographer, a soaring pilot, a mountain climber, and a multimedia consultant and producer.

Index